Wild

and
other stories of adventure

GW01269758

ANGIE BELCHER

photographs by Andy Belcher

Contents

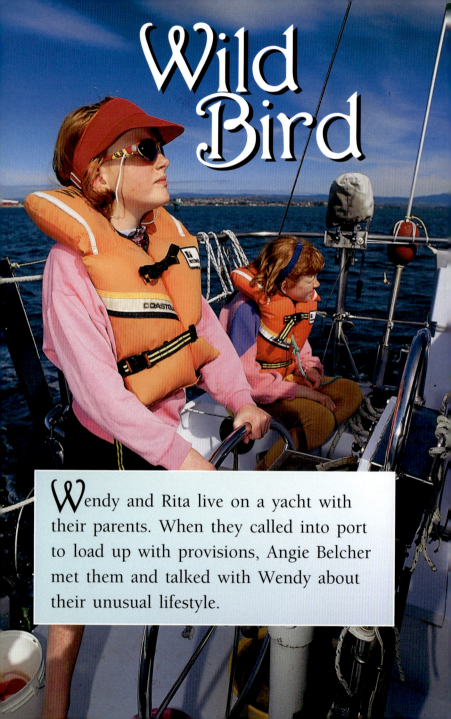

Wild Bird

Wendy and Rita live on a yacht with their parents. When they called into port to load up with provisions, Angie Belcher met them and talked with Wendy about their unusual lifestyle.

Our boat is our home. Like the whales and dolphins, we're always on the move. We used to live in a house, but Mum and Dad felt the call of the sea and set sail.

It can be cramped living on a boat. Our yacht, *Wild Bird*, is not big at all – 12.6 metres long and 4 metres wide. I can eat my cereal, clear the table, and wash the dishes without having to take more than six paces!

Keeping everything shipshape is not a problem – "There's a place for everything and everything must be in its place." We have one tiny drawer each, and we all share the only wardrobe. It measures just three hand spans across and six hand spans down.

In our bedroom, every bit of space is used. We even share the one large bunk. Sometimes we argue about who should turn out the light or who's hogging all the blankets, but usually it's fun.

Even on a boat, you can't get away from school work, especially when you have a mum and a dad who are both teachers! Mum tells my school which ports we'll be calling at, and they send our lessons to the nearest post office.

School starts at nine o'clock and goes on until midday. We always study the country or area we're visiting. In Fiji, we visited the villages and learned about how the people lived there. In Tonga, we went diving in the lagoons to study the sea life, and we went whale watching.

After lunch, we have free time. We read, play music, do our hobbies – and sometimes argue! Living together for twenty-four hours a day can be hard. I try to get my own space by going to the bow to look for whales or dolphins. Rita goes to the opposite end of the boat.

Before we set off on a long ocean voyage, we buy a huge amount of groceries. Our shopping list begins like this: 144 eggs, 12 blocks of cheese, 98 toilet rolls, 20 tins of beans, 30 kilos of flour, 15 kilos of sugar, and so on. We can easily fill five supermarket trolleys. But the shopping is the easy part.

Finding the space to store three months' groceries on board the boat can be difficult. Mum plans our meals very carefully, and we try not to eat all the yummy food first. Imagine spending the last two weeks of a voyage living on tinned peas and cereal!

Keeping food fresh is also a problem. We wrap potatoes in newspaper and coat eggs with grease. We don't have a freezer on board, so there's never any ice cream, frozen chips, or meat. But we do eat a lot of fresh fish, of course!

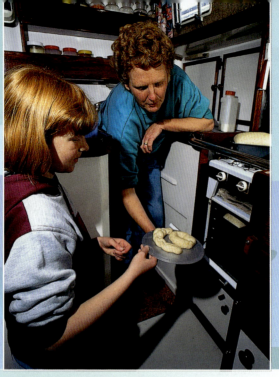

We love cooking in the galley, but it gets a little cramped. One day, the sink got blocked with food scraps. Mum tried to unblock it, but two little fish got sucked up into the pipes. We could hear them flapping away. When Dad unscrewed the pipe and shone the torch down, a pair of beady eyes stared up at him. Another time, a jellyfish came up into the toilet bowl!

Having a shower in such a small bathroom isn't much fun. The easiest way is to shower sitting on the toilet. The most important thing to remember is to take the toilet paper out before you start!

When the sea is rough, *Wild Bird* rocks around and makes me feel sick. When this happens, I lie on the bunk and try to think about nice things. Once, even that didn't work. I spent nine long days being sick. The only solid thing I ate was a small bowl of cereal. I hope I never have to go through that again.

But the best part of yachting is taking a turn at the helm. With the wind in my hair, dolphins skimming through the water in front of us, and the sound of the wind singing in the sails, I drift off into a dreamland. At times like this, I feel like I could sail to the end of the world.

Fly Like a Bird

For his birthday this year, Scott has asked for something a little different. He's always wanted to do a parachute jump to find out what it's like to fly through the air like a bird. And now, at last, he's going to get his wish.

Scott will do a "tandem" skydive. This means that he'll be harnessed to an instructor for the jump.

First of all, Mark, the instructor, dresses Scott in a jumpsuit. This will stop Scott's clothes flapping around in the air. Then he pulls a harness up over Scott's legs and across his shoulders. This is like a strong net that will keep Scott and Mark together for the jump.

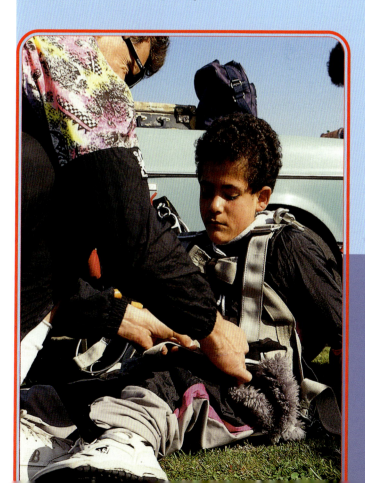

Mark lifts Scott up by the shoulder harness. "See how comfortable it feels," he says.

Scott puts on a soft leather helmet and a pair of goggles. Then he sits back in his wheelchair while Mark explains what will happen.

Next, Mark lifts Scott into the plane. They practise getting out of the plane's open door – it's not so scary when the plane's still on the ground!

It's time for take-off. Scott sits safely on Mark's lap as the plane rushes along the runway. A cool breeze rushes in through the gap where the plane's door used to be. Mark fits Scott's goggles so that he can look out of the door without the wind stinging his eyes.

Scott looks down. Everything looks so small, but he's not scared. He's just excited thinking about his first jump. The plane climbs up to 2500 metres. Scott can see the airport runway stretching like a ribbon below them.

"It's time," says Mark. He lifts Scott's legs out of the doorway, and they both wriggle forward. "Ready?" shouts Mark, as a rush of wind hits them. "Three, two, one … GO!"

Strapped together, they drop out of the plane. Their arms are stretched out like wings to stop them from turning and tumbling. A few clouds roll past as the seconds tick by. Now Scott knows what it feels like to fly like a bird.

As the ground gets closer, Mark pulls a tiny parachute out of his pocket and throws it behind them. This pulls the big parachute out of his backpack. It rustles and flaps as it fills up with air.

Suddenly everything slows down. They float silently towards the earth. When they get close to the ground, Mark pulls hard on the two steering lines, and they touch down safely on the ground.

Mark gives Scott a certificate that says he's done his first tandem skydive.

"What do you want for your next birthday, Scott?" he asks.

"Maybe I'll go for a scuba-dive," says Scott.

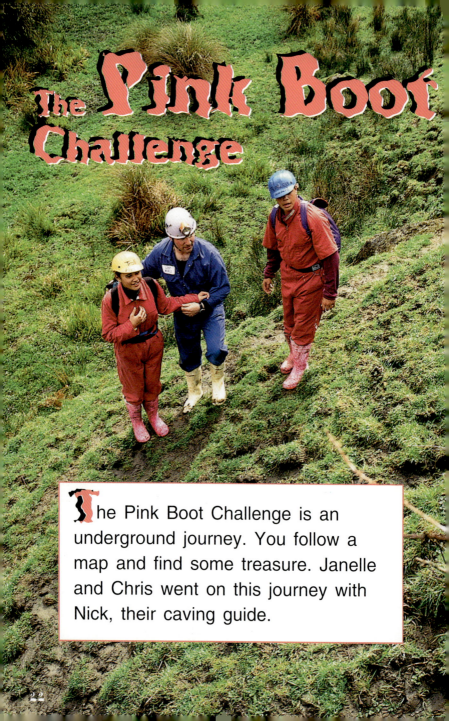

The Pink Boot Challenge

The Pink Boot Challenge is an underground journey. You follow a map and find some treasure. Janelle and Chris went on this journey with Nick, their caving guide.

"First, I need to make sure that nothing scares you," said Nick. He pointed to a small hole. "If you're going to come underground, I need to know you're not going to get scared climbing through small places."

Test result … we passed.

"OK, you'd better put these on."

"Pink boots!" said Chris.

"For luck," said Nick. "You'll need it. These caves are a bit scary. Strange noises … strange smells …"

I knew it was only talk, to make the adventure more fun … but I felt spooked.

Nick gave us each a helmet. Mine said **Troll Patrol** on the front. What did he take us for – a couple of kids?

"First you need to get the map from the troll hole," said Nick. Underneath a stone, we found an old piece of paper. **Black Bog of Eternal Stench**, it said, and **Lost Cave** and **Hidden Treasure**.

We set off for the Black Bog of Eternal Stench. "The only way across the bog is by flying fox," said Nick.

So over we went. So far, this was fun.

"Now for the cave," said Nick. "I've got my helmet light, and we've got a lantern each. And, of course, the ancient spitting rock from the Valley of Ving."

Chris looked at me and raised his eyes as Nick took a grey rock from his pack. "Spit on the rock of Ving," he said – so Chris did.

"Yuck!" I said. "Half of your breakfast was in that lot." But the rock was fizzing and bubbling. Then Nick lit a match, and the rock burst into flame. Shadows raced around the cave as we followed an orange ribbon down the black passage.

A stalagmite rose from the floor. On top of it sat a goat's skull! Stalactites hung from the ceiling.

A breeze blew through the cave. "What's that?" I asked. I kept telling myself this was just an adventure game.

"This cave breathes," said Nick slowly.

I shivered. I was scared, but I didn't want to let Chris know. Then Chris whispered, "I've got butterflies, Janelle. What about you?"

"No way!"

"Well, you go first, then!"

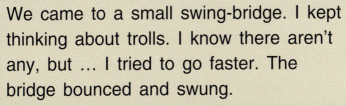

We came to a small swing-bridge. I kept thinking about trolls. I know there aren't any, but ... I tried to go faster. The bridge bounced and swung.

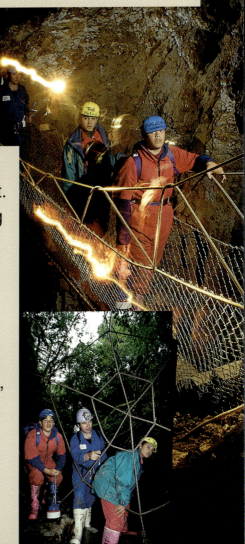

Ahead of us was sunlight. I ran for it. Across the opening was a spider web made of rope.

"The web of the giant spider," said Nick. "You have to climb through without touching it."

I laughed. Now that I could see daylight, I was OK.

I climbed through the ropes, then turned to watch Chris. He and Nick had disappeared! "Chris!" I yelled. "Don't mess around!" Now I was scared.

There was a faint yell. I ran through the trees. There was Chris, hanging up in another "spider web". I cut him free, and we followed the map to the mud slide.

The mud slide led into a narrow cave.

"You go first," I said.

"After you," said Chris.

We went together.

At the end of the cave was an old wooden box. "The treasure!" I said.

Then, "Bugs!" yelled Chris. "Hundreds of bugs!"

"You're not scared of a few bugs, are you, Chris?" I smiled.

We crawled back along the muddy floor, pushing the box in front of us. Then out into the fresh air.

Away from trolls.
Away from goats' skulls.
Away from bugs.

"We made it!" yelled Chris.
"That was fantastic, Nick," I said,
"even though there's no such thing as
a troll. Is there …?"

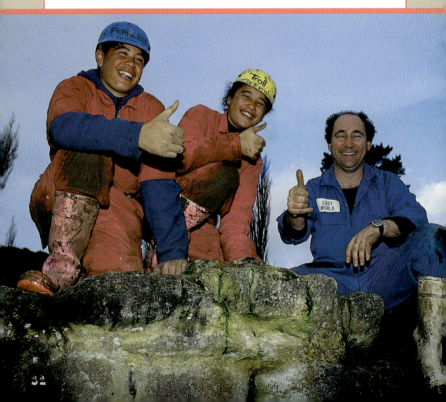